SYMMETRY

Ian Nimmo White

IAN NIMMO WHITE

2007

Cover Design: Kay Hunter

Book Design and Typesetting: Joy Hendry

Order this book online at www.trafford.com/07-1036
· or email orders@trafford.com

Most Trafford titles are also available at major online book retailers.

Printed in Victoria, BC, Canada.

ISBN: 978-1-4251-2929-3

www.trafford.com

North America & international
toll-free: 1 888 232 4444 (USA & Canada)
phone: 250 383 6864 ♦ fax: 250 383 6804
email: info@trafford.com

The United Kingdom & Europe
phone: +44 (0)1865 722 113 ♦ local rate: 0845 230 9601
facsimile: +44 (0)1865 722 868 ♦ email: info.uk@trafford.com

10 9 8 7 6 5 4 3 2

Contents

Foreword

Twa Tongues

When I look up my thesaurus, 'Symmetry' is the word which best appeals to me as an all-embracing synonym for balance, equilibrium or equanimity, and therefore a title which best symbolises the truce at long last declared in my mind between Scots and the English language.

For most of my life, in a wide variety of situations, I juggled with the dilemma of whether or not to use Scots. And always hovering over me was the spectre of English with its protruding, professorial nose. In part I use my unfair advantage as a poet in both disciplines to claim my present comfort with both languages, but I do feel, initially inspired by Gaelic getting out of jail, that we have enough confidence now to believe in the ability for Scots to take a credible flight-path – if not in parallel to English, at least in the same air space.

As a child I let loose in my mother tongue on emotional occasions – with family in celebration, heated discussion or quarrel – in street or school play with friends – as a spectator on the cinder terracing of Saint Mirren's football ground (What a roller-coaster that was!) – or simply cursing to myself at pain, ill luck or frustration. About the time of going to school, English was introduced or rather, imposed. I succumbed to the notion that if one was to 'get on in life' English was the most roadworthy vehicle and the more finely tuned it was, the better. Add a pinch of elocution and you could acquire 'the telephone voice' which if not a hearty sound wasn't half handy when it came to scoring points.

Much later in life, having been picked out as a poet by whatever power decides that, I used English as my medium without a second thought. After early struggles came a few years of modest publishing success. Then something strange happened. I started dabbling in Scots, for no apparent reason. Perhaps my childhood ramblings were being exhumed and reinvented by some supernatural force. Who knows?

Feebly at first, making mistakes like the crafting of dialect without due attention to phonetic detail, or sifting in random

9

English inappropriately, I pulled out all the 'Ah's and 'aa's, 'tae's and 'twa's, 'cuid's and 'cuidnae's, until I had something remotely akin to linguistic integrity and had developed some notion of what Scots was and what it had to offer to the 21st century reader.

No Scottish writer worthy of the name would claim such a thing as definitive Scots, no matter how many dictionaries are to hand – precious few in truth. And with all the movement of our people to find work within the UK and around the globe, it's hard to believe in distinctive dialects any more. Thankfully they do prevail, read if you will the lyrical, sprightly Shetlandic or Norn of Christine De Luca, the rich and pithy Doric of Sheena Blackhall and the fastidious phoneticism of Tom Leonard's Glaswegian.

For my part I have evolved an ostensibly Scots route map of my travels, more accurately house removals – a fusion of Glaswegian, Border, Fife and Tayside. To further try the reader, when I discover an old clinker of a word, whatever its origins I'll throw it in because it sounds so damn good. Luckily, although there have been few outlets for work, I've had understanding and eclectic editors, especially John Law of *Lallans* to whom I'm eternally grateful.

This might not sit easy with the purist, but for myself I'm happier with a Scots which I feel will be comprehensible to as wide an audience as possible in a fast and ever-changing world. Recently, in the course of a day's stroll around Edinburgh's bookshops, I struck up short conversations with at least ten individual young people. I'm lucky if I can remember half of them as natural born Scots. So I'm swayed by the slogan: *one Scotland, many cultures.*

When it comes to English, I go with MacDiarmid's thinking. It's a great language. And it's done a great deal for me. My early inspiration for poetry came from Scottish poets writing exclusively in English – Norman MacCaig and Douglas Dunn. And as a first time failure at Higher English when just a schoolboy, I get no end of a kick from being recognised nowadays as a sculptor in one of its highest forms, thumbing my nose as I go at the ghosts of old teachers.

As for why I opt for one tongue or t'other when a poem's 'coming in', I've no idea. Sometimes, when I'm feeling humorous, it's Scots. Sometimes, when I'm terribly serious, it's English. That at least says something about a Scot's keen and natural grasp of mischief. If any readers are disappointed at the ratio of English to Scots poems being hardly symmetrical, my apologies, but whilst there are many outlets for publishing English verse, there are a mere handful for Scots by comparison.

And at the outset I made the decision, in the interests of those who matter most, the readers, to include only previously published work, that is to say work which had been objectively judged by my peers to be of good standard.

Dunn and MacCaig have already been mentioned. There are however a host of poets and poetry people without whom I wouldn't be this far. To mention them all would be inevitably unfair, for one would be missed out. I've played safe and selected a few friends and two groups who stand out: poet Maureen Macnaughtan, who co-edited *Fife Lines* with me and was the first writer reading my work to see some potential; my wife Janice who, as a professional librarian, adds insight to the business of second guessing the reader, and as my severest critic is my best ally; Joy Hendry of *Chapman*, the eternal perfectionist, whose publishing experience was crucial to the design of this book, and Kerry Wilson who did a fine artwork job on the cover. Then there are the many friends in poetry who have worked, or gathered as poets, at the Scottish Poetry Library in Edinburgh and have helped in all sorts of ways to ensure I never felt on my own. Lastly, the tax payers of Fife who afforded me the job of professional youth and community officer for thirty five years. Working with them and their families gave me an appreciation of the realities and hopes of their lives, consequently a deeper understanding of myself, and in the final years priceless material for many of my verses. Poetry is not primarily the product of a literary mind. It's a stab at the truth, and at its best a moving and convincing one.

Ian Nimmo White, Leslie, Fife, 2007

Acknowledgements

The author wishes to express his gratitude to the literary editors / officers of the following magazines, newspapers and organisations for first publishing the poems in this collection:

The Broken Fiddle

Cencrastus

The Coffee House

Eclipse

The Herald

Krax

Lines Review

Never Bury Poetry

Northwords

Poetry Scotland

Scottish Arts Council

The Scottish Poetry Library

Cadenza

Chapman

Cutting Teeth

The Eildon Tree

Iota

Lallans

Markings

New Writing Scotland

Pennine Ink

The Scots Magazine

Scottish Book Trust

Understanding

Poems in English

Requiem

He's on my right shoulder today,
going on about Bradman's triple hundred,
the history of cagebirds and how,
if it hadn't been for him and such
as him, Herr Hitler would have won.

He'll·turn to his garden and dig,
breaking down frustration,
burying Malta and Murmansk,
and building opportunity for me
in his head. Endlessly digging.

She's on my left shoulder,
playing the part of *Serena Meek*
in Paisley Amateur Dramatic Society's
Lord Richard in the Pantry. She'll take
three curtain calls with me stood
embarrassed and proud
in short trousers and knee-length socks.

Next day, she'll treat me to lunch
in a posh restaurant. She'll talk
of Mrs Pankhurst and Greta Garbo,
while smoking cigarettes in style.

This was mere drama to me:
I wanted the world.
It didn't seem much to ask for.
I reckoned it wouldn't take long.

Primal

Tall trees stand guard
along the perfect firebreak
where a summer evening strolls.

Although the motorway retreats,
shafts of muffled noise
still hang around

till leaves are heard
to shiver in a play
of sunset light and shadow.

Below, the branding marks
of blackened twigs, ash
crushed and bruised, betray

a passion that still smoulders.
No landlord ever walks
this otherworldly place,

where deer must dart
or pheasants rise
to reinstate the present.

White-out

This snowscape has an orange skin at dawn.
It rings of eternal Sunday.
I am a dot on a white country
and hear only its numberless hymn.

The present is still. No-one is working.
The future ceases to be important.
History becomes a confidante,
catalogued in rows of white shelving.

I make tracks for the crystal trees,
where mini-avalanches
are thumping down from tired branches.
With boots submerged and absorbent knees,

I am that pathetic human animal,
chewing on air, limbs askew,
left dead by the dog, the athlete, who
leaps like a salmon from hole to hole.

I swim to the shelter of the house
to add one more soaking pair
of socks to the uniform line, and stare
through the melting window, till news

comes with crisis and forecast.
Tomorrow the thaw will drive its path
with a slow but telling truth:
this solitude was not meant to last.

Consecration

End of studies, Friday night *flicks*,
half back for the school eleven
next morning, moving on
to boo and cheer Saint Mirren

in the afternoon. Some friend of a friend's
would be free for a beer
and with luck a smooch on Saturday night.
All those teenage passions

anti-climaxed down on Sunday mornings:
the *Post*, the *People*, the *Express* and *Mail*
exchanged and combed
from front to back or as you please

in a sitting-room turned library
– a family's weekly round-up,
the feisty five in huddled hush,
all eyes glued to the holy writ.

Only a puff from rounded lips
parting pages stuck together
or a fly in screaming nosedive,
a half finished breakfast in his sights,

could infiltrate the *shtoom*!
– a busy household's secular prayer
in mortgage-paying post-War Scotland.
Who'd dare break the solemn ring?

The quiet could be so consummate,
it took on lifeform, hummed a bit,
up the flu and in the walls,
made teacups ring and dentures click.

The epic rag was therapy.
Behind it wrath was muffled and doused.
So what St Mirren had lost again?
Domestic rebounds stumped me as a boy.

Though three are gone, it's strange
how clear I see them reading still,
cover to cover as they all warmed down
from a life though simpler just as full.

Kirkforthar

The sun trickles through calligraphy
on the pine-tops and the path
becomes a chess board of dark and light,
a swithering of midges
one moment there, the next,
no more, illusion performed.

A train shaves the edge of the tree-line,
shooting towards Dundee, its long
drawn out ebb more of a wind
than a wind now knelt in prayer
in this green and grand cathedral;
then only a roe deer, surprised,

will shatter silence, beating retreat
on dead wood, tree-root and tussock;
or a woodpecker with his rapid tattoo
at the start of work. It finishes
in a portico of light, which bottles
all of the business of beyond.

Paisley Cobbler

Hmm was all that he would say,
or could say, the spikes
of his nails arranged
in a row between his teeth.
I used to count them – *seven today.*
His shirt-sleeves screwed nut-tight,
veins out like cable wiring,
the last sang to his blows.
At the threaded chimes of eleven,
he sat down in his thoughts
and took his break – pieces first,
then the tea. In all I had waited
an hour for his acknowledgement:
Are you doing all right at school?
Half way through my answer,
he was back in rhythm.
Time was money. I didn't mind.
My grandfather communicated
well enough in his own way.

Tea and Scones

There was a kettle on the burner
whistling for attention,
a *Marconiphone* was squawking in the corner
– losers when it came to competition:

Auntie Jenny filled the sofa
bringing all her latest on the Street
The lass at 23's due in September,
the lad at 36 will do what's right.

The best of china on parade,
regimental, pristine white,
tea pouring from the spout at giddy height.
A scone with butter? Marmalade?

Auntie's fearsome tittle-tattle
moved her teeth around her mouth.
the dog sat still, transfixed, beneath,
working out just when his share would fall.

I had one ear glued to the wireless
(Cliff Richard's *Livin' Doll*),
the other plugged with liquorice,
fresh out were we of cotton wool.

But the yackety-yak went on and on.
Sister Lizzie went next door,
and while Mum maintained a stoic air,
played Beethoven briskly on piano.

The dog gave up all hope.
With front paws on his temples
and the longest weary howl,
fell backwards on the carpet, belly up.

The old wagging clock chimed four.
You could cut the mass relief.
The children were so good Auntie inferred.
Same time next week my lambs?
                            Good grief!

Monday Mornings

An owl saves one hoot
for signing off his shift,
while I could not give two
for the one directly after it.

Like Friday's sour milk
the night moon hangs around,
as day begins to feel
the way it looks and sounds.

There's a strangeness of good manners
in a soporific flow
of traffic not road raged
or jammed – wilfully just slow,

while poker-faced pedestrians
criss-cross without a blether
in metronomic step
and Outer Space demeanour.

Passing the ten pound note
for a thirty pence tabloid
draws a forced "No trouble, sir"
from a face much underjoyed

and dropping the kids at school
is done without a 'bye-ee'
– to the sound of slamming doors
and a back-to-the-grindstone sigh.

Hebridean Selkies

Their heads are set like busts,
rock steady on the waterplinth.
Is this the reason
one million shorebound galleries
have dubbed them *People of the Sea*?

They would have watched in wonder,
when Haakon heaved his longboats South
to settle sway with Alexander,
at fierce war-churning bipeds,
all horns and jagged edges.

They must have known despair,
when shedding skin to mate
and splice that jingoistic gene,
to see young machos, slow of thought,
miss out then turn to stone.

Look to your own, Selkie:
from your seaweed-cushioned rock,
behold your mate as he explodes
from the myriad of sea-bed kelp,
loops up to dive and head-bang water.

Be enticed.
Let slide.
Dissolve.

Love and Dishes

Whilst drying dishes,
I hypothesised on who
murdered JFK.

You demanded that I
wipe the jam jar before
putting it away.

This resulted in a row
on the scale of
a nuclear explosion.

Which was more important
– the whodunnit or the jar?
Answer: neither.

But both together
concoct the fuel you need
to keep a fire burning.

The Dam at Nethy Bridge

In a crystal pool three builders
swarm all over the task,
minds hives of invention,
their backs sun-pinked and polished.

In his gifted swim, the dog
rudders towards them
and beavers a log
in and out of a pause for thought.

Through the clear shifting water,
a marbled bed
reflects the light and evening
yawns above the magnetic flow.

With each momentous gain
comes a whoop of kept delight,
their bodies flailing backwards
the way a salmon leaps.

Soon, chittering teeth call time
and arms in a 'W',
little men under hooded towels
go into informed debate

on the science of water resistance.

Shades of Van Gogh

Close to the harvest fields, my hair
thickening in smoke, a confetti
of lapwings whirled, striking
at air again and again:
p-weet   p-weet   p-weet.

A pheasant craked in callous pines
at a shot slung out
of a man with no face.
A wood pigeon packed
its wings away and,

kissing the sky goodbye,
raised its undercarriage
to crash in reels of hay.
A unanimity of *p-weets*
detonated in my head.

Is This Really Scarborough?

This cloak's not on for long,
intermezzo of sea's
barbaric breath in deck-chair ease,

engulfing beach then street
then park, transforming all things
stone or still to shrouds.

A queue of blinded cars
goes canny down a hill,
each brakelight winking, *Copy me.*

Nostalgic *Lara's Theme*
is the dauntless ice cream van; and
funfare lights, now whorled haze,

draw notice to themselves alone.
Below them, children's voices plot,
released from all control.

Elsewhere, there's nothing
to take in, just one lone dancer,
once more having moved

serenely from the wings
and with economy of steps,
crossed the stage to make sharp exit.

Teenagers

These days I pass them on the stairs,
at noon when they surface
or midnight
when they all but demolish the door.

If it occurs, conversation
is monosyllabic
– anonymity's cool and
I'm (*The Invisible Man*).

There are strange forces at work:
carpets crawl with dirty
dishes and disowned clothes;
when the music (?) starts,

I could be in the waiting room
of the dentist's
or in the Tropics,
a mosquito in my ear.

This is not the home
I helped create
– a spaceway service station,
half way stop on planet Zog.

I'll push off to a croft
and write my poems in peace,
until they all arrive,
oddly articulate and caring

and seriously short of cash.

Cutting Roots

In this strangely unfamiliar house,
I get a sense of company
when treading on bare floorboards.

On the last carpet to lift
are the stains of Hogmanays and
neighbours' visits. None a stranger here.

The air is bruised with stale
and stubborn nicotine, shades
of in-smoking days and elegance.

No wall-clock, just a pencilled outline.
A tarnished bowling trophy, all
that is summer grass and evening.

And, overseeing operations
from its customary perch,
the wooden owl. It once took wings

– was thrown at me in temper,
missing and crashing through glass
to meet an astonished postman.

The kettle blows to its punctual click
– medicinal tea, a letter
to pick up, they haven't heard.

Then past the heavy blossomed
cherry tree we planted, and on
to wife, children and new growth.

The Work Ethic

That's the Town Hall clock.
Is it striking one or four?
The security light next door's
going on and off, and on and off.
Is this what Alcatraz was like?

A startling shower of rain
gushes like a river in spate,
bringing brief serenity.
And one year on, a milkcart
jingles into Purgatory.

The sheet is strangulated.
Someone else's pulse
is pounding in the pillow.
This bugger's locked inside the brain
turning like a hamster driven wheel.

Never go home on a grudge
a wise old boss once said.
Fat chance this time. It makes you
want to murder whatever the cost.
Three ways have been explored this night.

There goes the morning alarm. It's Nature's
gift. Two hours of unremembered bliss.
Back to the fray and a making-up
with a *none intended* and of course
none taken exchange.

Five Shopping Days till Christmas

The family being no longer young,
a Christmas tree was picked without care
almost as an afterthought this year.

Out of its net it would not straighten
and tattered books were to find a place
under one leg of the tripod base.

Last year's lights proved faulty too.
Not long before the shoppers lost cool
then, one for the other, the season's good will.

More by chance the job got done
and all sprawled out destroyed in chairs.
For one full hour their thoughts were theirs,

until the one who'd started it all
let out with a smile: *I like this bit.*
Sat here in darkness when the tree's first lit.

Once More with Feeling

When mornings never seem to rise
and streetlamps play time-tricks on eyes,
it's time for people, unabashed,
to wear a hat, get stuffed, get smashed.

Xmas for most is a feeling and thought
of times and places in which they were taught
of reindeer and stocking, patience and wish,
a yo-ho-hos white beard and tache.

But now the mall is a merry-go-round
seething with entrepreneurial sounds,
jingling the latest sledgehammer reduction
on last year's rejected and mothballed collection.

Being a chauvinist I do my bit
and go for a bird in a last minute hit,
trapped in a frenzy of like-minded souls
in a freezer click-clunking with cold cannonballs.

Hot or cold turkey, slice after slice,
devotion to dumplings, sultanas and spice,
brussel sprouts, roasters, an overweight race
packing the lot where there ain't no more space.

I get my kicks with a tipple or two – okay, three
from that wee special somethin' kept locked under key.
Then, flat on the sofa, out of harm's reach,
I can snore and miss out on the 3 o'clock speech.

Lonesome Johnny

He went fasting after work
to the place he called 'Church'
– a whiff of stale beer,
the jingle of a crate,
always the doorstep to sanctuary.

He mounted a stool – his stool,
where informed barmaids
served up without asking
and won his first smile of the day.
The long devotions then began.

A fruit machine chuckled at a loser
who wouldn't let go. Holding court,
young men bragged about conquest.
In a conclave old men exchanged pathos
and new frames of pool added thunder.

Nothing distracted his fix
on the gallery of optic and liqueur
– a CV he never regretted,
so long since he'd given absolution
to a sober duplicitous world.

I was never to see him at night
in his self-imposed seclusion,
(The lesser of evils he described it)
– only on antiseptic mornings,
when his hands made full disclosure.

Committee

In broken-down and windy public halls
where the heating's always ice-cube cold,
unlikely trawls of democrats
crank up man's finest ever machine
for argie-bargie and indecision-making.
Ten minutes in, still inquorate,
the limelight falls on Mrs Smith
who's just been made a granny first time round.
We shouldn't scoff. It could well be
the only stimulation
this side of tea and biscuits and goodnight.
That grumpy old caretaker muscles in:
Last time the chairs were not put back
and twenty dirty teacups left unwashed.

With apologies and intimations,
amendments moved, unmoved, unmended,
you'll check the time in disbelief. You'll wish
you'd stayed before the Box
to watch Real Madrid v. Man. United.
What's been done to death before
is exhumed with equal vigour
to be unresolved and buried one more time.

Any Other Business? cries the Chair.
The silly sod. He's asked for it now,
as seven fresh contentions hit the table.
Dear Scottie, please return and beam me up.
We could well be here till midnight,
barring power cut, flash flood or missile
locking on to this dynamic source of heat.
Thank God there's still one antidote:
Someone boil a kettle. Who's for tea?

A Skeleton Steps out of the Cupboard

In the tedious hum and hush
of a sleepless slow-river night,
when a room under siege
has been sucked clean of air
and the brain is a minute hand
for the time between tolling of bells,

a scream in the middle distance,
the final rasping choke
of survival's unfittest, is the fuse
for the now undisguised, undressed,
and unimportant one
to look inward and reprise

the untold, untellable tale.
Around and around it goes
like a complex play by Shakespeare,
the lead in several roles
from an unashamed ruthless lion
to a guilt-ridden penitent mouse,

with the stock predictable ending
and the same unnourished
audience of one.

But morning's nitty-gritty light
will once more dress and rehearse
our hero for the day to come.

Exposure and Re-acquaintance

An arresting stillness on waking
reveals that a great white duvet
has laid itself down in the night.
Impulsively, a neighbour's child

waves to me from her window,
not something she'd normally do,
as the radio broadcasts her freedom
and that of ten thousand peers.

Motorists, bound to be late,
shuffle snow and say *dreadful*
(that cultured lie). We Northerners
pretend we don't enjoy our struggles,

our spades, the huff and puff of it;
children on remembered sand,
constructing channels from the sea
to sturdy castles fit for siege;

sportsmen of a bygone age,
grooving out a natural rink
for curling, shades of L S Lowry,
black against the bleakest white.

All schemes well laid postponed,
rejigged or booted out. And yet,
with no great harm to mice nor men,
return to routine somehow new.

Mrs Nimby Says

The local council want to build
a youth club here I've heard.
It's right the young should be fulfilled
But ... not in my back yard.

You pull 'em up, they say "Up yours!"
and stare you in the eye.
I think a Centre's just the cure
though ... N - I - M - B - Y.

They look like death, their music's loud,
the language makes you sigh.
Take them in, the whole mad crowd
but ... N - I - M - B - Y.

Sex and drink, a damn disgrace,
drugs both soft and hard.
Still, the young must have their place
though ...

Not in my back yard.

Unlikely Hero

Two years after John Adams had murdered Matthew Quintal, Edward Young died of asthma. It was Christmas Day 1800. Adams was now the only surviving member of the nine mutineers on HMAV Bounty who had found Pitcairn Island in 1790 and the only adult male now living there. The next male in the pecking order was Thursday October Christian, son of Fletcher and Maimitti, only 10 years old. Having been taught to read and write by Young, Adams turned to Christianity, giving the island stability and the surviving Polynesian/English offspring a glimmer of hope.

In 1808, when the world discovered the Pitcairn colony, Adams learned that Bligh and the entire crew of the longboat, cast adrift by the mutineers on that fateful day in 1789, had survived the long haul to Timor. When finally pardoned by The British Navy in 1814, he at last enjoyed some peace of mind before dying in1829 at the age of 65. The colony survives to the present day and is known as Adamstown.

On two square miles
of genetic guilt

an unkept stone
lies in a thicket

to one and one only
founding father,

born into want,
illiterate thief,
predestined jack tar,

mutineer, survivor,
murderer turned pastor,
builder of refuge,

preserver of life.

Scriptorium

This is something I climb into.
Not a vehicle, no wheels, no engine.
Not a hiding place, no treehouse.
There's no door or wall or roof,
no measurable dimension.

No clocks tick here. There are
no deadlines or appointments.
With only an image for ignition,
this is a motionless
rollercoaster of a journey.

Cares uncannily melt away.
No longer husband, father, brother.
And yet all three the better on return.
A holiday can't match it. Paradise
taboo to travel agents.

Imagination's canvas
widens to embrace
a new and legal lexicon.
It's fun to dig up
dead English teachers, show them up!

I can be pulled from it. At home
with *Thought you were doing the dishes.*
At work: *You haven't yet submitted
your outcome, input, output data.*
Mostly, I get left alone.

A black hole here on Earth
where fear, real or of itself,
has zero impact. Comfort zone
for one still seeking the truth,
well knowing he'll never find it.

The Searing Yellow Leaf

(In-service Training)

This present devotion to physical fitness
is all very healthy and mostly light-hearted.
It's shared by all ages and shapes of fanatics,
till one clown gets pushy and others get baited.

My tatty old track suit came out of the closet
and throttled a stomach for years overfed.
One look at the circuit and I knew I was past it,
held fast on the spot by a breath-sucking dread.

The coach, who was built like a New Zealand prop,
was steeped in a sergeant's distinctive finesse:
If ye like it, then run till ye bloody well drop.
If no, ye can lump it, Ah cuidnae care less.

Some in ash coloured sannies that sounded like clogs,
some sweating profusely in swill-bellied vests,
some digging the line like the hind legs of dogs,
but for glory of section, all stuck out their chests.

I was proud of old Billy who fairly took off,
so game, so fit and so dandy.
His tubular legs were now strutting their stuff,
as Dan McPhail's pistons would show Para Handy.

A young buck now left me for dead doing ninety
with a body to kill for and blond flowing mane.
My hurt pride then made me aggressively nifty,
which won me a searing centrifugal pain.

Three laps on we ran into a shower.
It afforded a minute's refreshing relief.
Then a skullcap burst forth like a broken down gutter
and soaked its incumbent right through to his briefs.

I caught up a chap who'd now had it
– a man of the cloth, he'd knelt down for a prayer.
When I stopped to give comfort, he muttered:
Take me now and release me, dear Father.

The coach called us in for tuition:
Not in my life – Oh what crap – Ye're pathetic!
I implored his promotion to Omega10
where Klingons pull toe-nails without anaesthetic.

My poor legs have lost their persuasion.
I walk like a cowboy. I've run out of time.
I feel more upbeat in my versification
where feet are for metre, aerobics for rhyme.

Walking Round Holl Reservoir

In evening's understated grace
when the rain has come and gone,
stoic anglers on the Holl

continue their unclocked routines,
and an ageless West Lomond Hill
is a fresh green, brown and gold.

We go clockwise, anti-clockwise
(either way). And wind-combed
grass, bush, leaf and bloom

is the rhythm by which we keep
in step and hopefully harmony.
We listen to the rush of sluice water,

halt at the shriek of a heron
rising to span the reservoir
with a measured beat of its wings,

surprise a rabbit in the open,
frozen for a second then vanishing
down something no-one could find.

We do this for the exercise,
and the rest is left unsaid.
On the final straight we hug

the dam wall where the ground at our feet
falls through wood and farmland,
town and park, to the Forth beyond.

Back in the car, we turn the key
when shadow has raided West Lomond
and the anglers reel in the light.

High Street, Edinburgh

Here, in the centre of the centre,
at the crossroads of mentalities,
an old bibber climbs a steep hill,
with both arms grasping
for holds on the air
to counter the pull of gravity,

and harling the gaps between people
with pathos and berating.
Some look on with amusement,
some with pity or disdain.
Others catch in the lifeless eyes
mirrors for their own thinking.

How daft the world looks
in all its fake sobriety,
wearing a starched suit to hang
the plausible on insecurity,
and charting a zigzag course
around the truths of our time.

Sometimes It Happens That Way

My mind is out on safari today,
exploring as seldom before,
pushing out creative limits.

Who knows? I might encounter
a different type of *homo sapiens*,
new philosophy, another tongue.

Fact is I'm on the sickie. My arm's
in a sling. *Tendonitis* said the doctor,
take a rain check for two weeks.

I asked her what that meant
in terms of treatment and prognosis.
She wrote a lot and talked to her computer.

Doctors never fuss about my health.
She did say not to drive, I was *a danger*
Maybe they fuss over others.

Anyway, it's time to make the best of it.
The world has walked its dog. The letterbox
has played its one percussioned note.

I'll speak to my retired neighbour.
Both of us will have forgotten
we fell out over nothing years ago;

go to the post office, tell that sod
who's always peeved at my demands
for stamps he needs to get out more;

find out what it's like
to be cursed at and half-killed
by motorists, and yet feel more alive.

What if it doesn't last? if there's a call
to arms – to supermarket shopping
– to that procrastinated washing machine?

No danger. I'll wear my stereophonic
headset, cos I've trained myself
to hear the Muse with one ear

and listen to my fellow earthlings
with the other, while remembering
to nod at all those empathetic moments.

No, since you ask, it never
fools my love. Long since she's turned it
to advantage: *He'll say yes at any price*

Don't know what to do with myself.
Nor do I care. The clocks have lost their tick.
I can live like the dog and better –

– eat whatever and when I like;
sit in my garden, play guessing games
with birdsong; see a butterfly

as an open coloured book
or a stringed and silent instrument
stood upright in shapely splendour.

Enough is enough. There's something to do.
It seldom comes so quick. Look sharp.
It's almost there, so write it down.

Of Independent Mind

George Orwell (1903-1950)

The Burmese peasant, who fathomed little
of his trial, was hung in public by the British Raj.
A witnessing young officer, turning writer overnight,
scored it: *worse than a thousand bloody murders.*

Eric Blair signed off, took his TB down the mines,
and wrote in the slums of cities built around them:
Those who live right well above the ground
owe those who work bent double well below it.

All power to the pen and par for the course
for one who had to know that he might tell it:
freedom fighter in the Spanish Civil War,
took a bullet in the neck for telling content.

Radical scribe without a party card,
foe of Big Brother, friend of Havenot.
No pacifist: *Only the armament*
of the oppressed will shift the tyrant.

Showed that pigs and human beings
behaved alike given absolute power.
So what that 1984 has come and gone?
It happened before that. It will again.

Died of lesions from his childhood plague,
unmourned by the powers that be.
Rest easy, George. For yours are classics,
bequests of truth and vigilance.

Great Asby

(part of *Postcards from the Lake District*)

The gate just a tad off its hinge
is lifted then opened
with a shriek that chills the spine.

And the bleating goes on unnoticed,
for this is the sole pervading note
in a symphony of silence.

We dawdle downhill to the pub
through a village built from Pennine stone
and polished by a Pennine sun.

After a tipple, a platoon of ducks
paddle upstream to the bridge,
but someone's forgotten the bread.

No loss. By sunset on the upland
a convalescent lamb
is milked from a baby's bottle.

Before the Threshers Come

In the complacency of August
beside the tall and upright fields,
I stroll inevitably
some twenty giant paces
behind my youngest son:

all of eighteen harvests,
striding urgently, to catch up
with his thinking, doesn't see
the swaying ears of wheat
or hear the swallows switching.

Laggardly, with time to grasp
how Nature's changes
arrive with few surprises,
I pan around
this far-flung full-grown gold

two weeks before the threshers come.

Town Square Cafe

Like buses they arrived and departed
– a ten minute break in shopping,
time to top up on a cuppa.

Only crockery chatted, a chair
grunted back, grunted forwards
– a handy if not hearty place.

Excuse me darlin said an old lady
with one arm in a sling
Can you open my sugar for me?

How could I refuse? I replied
Best chat up line I've had in years
I tore the top off the paper sachet.

I take four, very sweet, like you
the octogenarian purred.
We swapped more compliments.

With the teensy lollipop stick
I stirred her tea. She went on
Long ago I had a one-armed boss.

Got maimed in The Great War.
Didn't stop him. A champion golfer.
But couldn't slice the top off a boiled egg.

I laughed. She giggled in triumph.
We had good crack as avant-garde
alfresco passed us by.

Going Grey

I like my hair trimmed
by a female hairdresser:

the perfumed water, creams,
and working so close,

the unavoidable
yet unexpected contact

– low voltage and prolonged
sensation, like way back

when my mother searched
painstakingly

for nits. But nowadays
and in this bustling place,

it's all too quickly over.

In the Shadow of Empowerment

I am elevated down ten floors
from a world of constant change,
and transported, by one green man,
to a different galaxy.

There are forty men in this place.
Not strictly true. Three women
shuttle-run the bar
to serve the thirty-seven.

As a shapely figure bends to sums,
a short skirt climbs a thigh
and oglers mentally compete
for homage when she spins.

Imitation wood, finger-touch pumps
and bland conglomerate decor
does nothing to disturb
the sense of *déjà vu*.

There is policy here enough,
unwritten but understood,
at the *Hard Luck* watering hole
where lines are single, Bogartian,

where the laughs they win
are a buffalo chorus, where need
is the mother of acceptance
and the time-served undertow

is challenge indeed
for the gifted wordsmiths of change,
high up and well-heeled
in their breeze block towers.

55 Not Out

As I go for a *Scotsman* this morning,
I'm feeling two insoles taller.
My significant other

has launched my 55th birthday
with an extra large top,
a book of selected Scottish verse,

and the kind of card that takes
more than five minutes to find,
says without saying it's meant.

Nothing from my offspring yet.
They'll get round to it. After all,
they live for kicks, not history.

Much later, one sleepyhead will note
the solitary card and utter
a loud four letter regret.

Another will find out on phoning
with all his troubles and his
current current account balance.

Today I'm at one with the World.
My application for an early exit
did dwindle into nothing.

But I'm not complaining. Too old
to be described as ageing,
too young to need a bus pass.

This milestone comes with privilege.
I can be snooty with a younger boss,
as he approaches

on a carpet of broken glass,
in a cute mismatch
of authority and dis-ease.

Still younger colleagues find me fun,
a curiosity, a fond respect.
My anecdotes and cracks

have them whirling in great glee
on swivel chairs. I ought to charge
for entertainment, make a kill.

If I'm stopping on, I'll invent
another mischief, stay a fly
in the ointment. But not today

on this my day of days.
I'm body swerving
all those broken dreams,

counting all my plusses,
what I have and better hold –
a love unwrapped and absolute.

Two Women

Fighting wind, the clock and fate,
she bulldozed up Croftouterly brae
a wide twin buggy and its sleeping weight.

Drawing breath she stopped to blether.
I listened to her spitfire tale
of job and college and steep childcare.

I thought to offer sympathy
then switched to a nodding smile:
She seems to feel it's better this way.

As they pushed off into the morning blue,
a curl of chimney smoke minded me
of a tenement flat in '52

where a mother blinded by onion mist,
in one square yard of scullery,
spun like a planet on its axis.

There in all her pot-pourri
was she saying through those clenching teeth:
It will be better for us one day?

Believe What You Will

From ignorance our comfort flows,
the only wretched are the wise

– Mathew Prior

Nothing barred at the discobar
– young guys impaled by studs and spikes
– young gals not into weather forecasts
wearing dishtowels top and tail.

One ageing foursome, three sheets
and more to the wind, were set
for a game of famous films and leading men:
Braveheart, Mel Gibson! First and last

points scored, the game now drowned
in 'Flower of Scotland' and 'Scots Wha Hae'.
Freedom's sword was strongly drawn
on Bannockburn and Buckfast.

Ooh, when the French lass and him made luv!
said the low-slung dress with the Benidorm boobs.
From nearby came an erudite riposte:
A tour de force, the princess only two years old!

I knew the history was rough but not
the lesson. The boyfriend was offended.
The scholar had seen Service in the Falklands.
Glasses were demolished, tables levitated

in a swing hit miss old cowboy brawl saloon.
With a split lip from a handbag's glancing blow,
one wee chap made a cinematic exit
from a catflap at the bottom of the maul.

It stopped tout de suite when the well-tanned lassie
spilled out from her dress. The two historians
called quits, shook hands, concurred
Wallace had at least been drawn and quartered.

Ballindalloch Castle Gardens

We were heading for Grantown-on-Spey:
Shall we pop in here for a bit?
Why not? she replied. It was one
of those unplanned, uncertain stops.

Saved half the cost by missing out
the Castle. Baronial homes are all
the same. Made an original start
at a miniature railway, pushed

buttons like gamblers paralysed
by a fruit machine. Had four trains
going like hell fire simultaneously and never a crash.

The walled rose garden was a high prison,
but no desire for a quick escape
– countless blooms of every hue,
heady scents from tart to subtle.

Strolled on to a serenity of ponies.
At first they were indifferent,
then curious, then friendly, then
disappointed (no treats on offer).

On the Speyside Walk, the glassy
surface of Scotland's swiftest river
shivered to goose bumps in a wind
whipped up by birch and alder.

Time itself was on holiday,
so the afternoon was gone
as swift as the water, as slick
as the sleight of a conjuror's hand.

Eden is an anywhere place
on planet Earth. But it can't
be planned, only stumbled on,
out of luck, perhaps of need.

Of Wood and Flesh

OK my loyal wooden friend,
weighed down, worm-holed and doodled on,
I owe you a major service:

one loose-end day to shed and shred
three stones of bureaucratic fat,
unjamb a drawer or two,

go plumb the archive, rediscover
triumph, disaster, secret,
the photograph that says it all

– how old I've grown in the job,
the letter written in anger
– unsent and just as well,

the award won by a colleague
so gifted with the best to come,
a life cut short. Too sad.

At last. I can see the grain,
feel the smoothness. Wood is grand.
Like wine it fortifies with age.

There we are. How smart you look.
They'll shortly rid themselves of me,
but you'll do nicely yet.

As Ever, Loch Leven

A companion seat of wrought iron,
no backrest, elliptical,
aesthetically thought out, original,
marks the spot for best of views:
inscribed for a couple who stood here,
took it in. We don't sit down.
Somehow it seems taken.
It's mid July and a rainproof Summer
has brought about an early hairst,
some fields already yellow, tincture
of Van Gogh, the fishing boats
so stoic they too could have been painted.
Moving at speed between them
is a longboat rowed by royal stewards.
Their lady's at the stern in Tudor dress,
her hair hung down, no time for grace,
looking at the castle which held her,
and now just fifty strokes from Burleigh Sands.

Bound for Kinross, we reach a wooden bridge,
a sturdy bridge, a craftsman's bridge.
It says: *Don't just walk across.*
Lean on me awhile.
We count the radiating circles
engineered by jumping fish.
We'd like to watch them
till the fading light. And why not?
No-one's around and the castle
is the only man-made thing in sight.
We can travel back in time
from Elizabeth Second to Elizabeth First,
further still were we not hung up on Mary,
see land and sky pick up a pace
to quickly clock the span.
Should we be concerned
if going back through the turnpike gate
the motor car's not there?

An Essential Place

Tonight, in this unsettled summer,
black clouds are on manoeuvres
tramping on the hilltops,

a nearby company of pines
whipping up a fairish breeze
to seashore strength. But down

at the car park, that lady unloads
her five labradors again.
How they bound and run

in all directions
simultaneously, yet
return to centre on command.

And four telegraph poles ahead,
a tractor, neat as a matchbox,
maintains a perfect line and pace

amidst a turmoil of birds.

When Young Men Can Rest

It's a day's journey nowadays
from Kirkcaldy to Kohima.
The old chindit

made it in a second.
And with more control than a poet
he left out the details.

Not to be outdone,
I didn't push. I didn't try
to break the silences.

When I was captured
they put me in a field prison.
They thought I knew something.

Each time they'd finished with me,
they put me in a dark pit
without water for three days.

The veteran drummed his fingers
on the wooden arm of his chair:
Over the points, over the points!

This mini session was over.
I didn't cry. If he
could do it later, so could I.

Principia

This is as good as it gets – where prattling PCs,
chirping phones and the whole of workaday tedium
ceases to tick, where sound is a skylark,
shot from his tufted home, tuning his voice
as he flutters upward to his goal,
where a blood orange sun dips down
to the shoulder of West Lomond Hill,
shade sweeps across slope and farmland
as if time was rewinding at speed,
bracken and leaf murmur in rhythm
and wild flowers fragrantly surpass
any thoughtfully arranged bouquet:

when I cease to say I wish
I knew back then what I know now,
when it dawns on me I still don't know
and what's more it matters less and less.
Now, poetry is possible, if not damned likely,
and I'm glad the drive's still there
(though mindful there's still a way to go) .
So here I am, nursing it all maternally,
like component parts of a well cooked meal,
a delicate bonsai in changing weather,
blacks potted off their spot at snooker,
a car being reversed into just enough space.

As a play of sunlight and wind
burns my skin and sharpens feeling,
the duskening tresses of Falkland Hill
drop to a drowsy plain below
where the lights of Ladybank and Freuchie,
Auchtermuchty and Dunshalt,
are vigils of hand-held candles.
At times like these the patois comes
as swift, as easy, as unexpected snow,
and an ageless unrelenting Forth
flows as poetry from a place uncertain
to its ever shifting destiny.

Commitment

On a tortuous hillside track
a mucky farm-mobile
phut-phut-phutted past.

Second guessing the swings,
a collie rode pillion, his back
to the driver. With mouth agape,

his great tongue
oscillating, he watched
the land speed away to the sea.

In the lap of West Lomond
behind him and closing, his charges
scurried into a scrum,

as if in premonition
of a rigorous morning's drive
by the devil's own disciple.

Revelation

For those indebted to Harold Drew,
captain of HMS Manchester, Malta Convoy, August 1942

Her picture hung on the stairhead wall.
And our father, who came back from it,
wouldn't, or couldn't, tell it all.
Our childhood daydreams plugged the gaps.

And now at the touch of a button,
we get stumped by the opened secret,
in our living room armchairs
torpedoed by the truth:

On the fourth morning of unbroken nightmare,
a kiss from Mussolini's matelots
smacks the warship's engine room.
Her part in deliverance is over.

She's moving in an endless zero.
It's a short watch to first light
and one-sided Armageddon.
The skipper opts for survival,

each crewman with the choice – for shore
or open sea. He scuttles
twelve thousand tons of Rule Britannia
and with it his rank and name.

For the Navy's gold embroidered hats,
the book was not for bending.
But today on Malta's remembering harbour
a few old shipmates are gathering

in their dwindling longevity
and satellite TV celebrity.
Among the flowers and brass band oompahs
they steal a moment's solitude

for private grief and gratitude.
How stiff and measured is judgement.
How swift and merciless
the dispassionate sea.

Oh, It Makes You Want To ... !

He's on a deadly cocktail from Buckfast to Black Mamba.
Football's Hyde is off on his bi-annual meander.
He's looking for a *Frog* to splat or a sour *Kraut* who's game
for an international one on one and morning tabloid fame.

From La Manche to Mississippi,
                        from the Thames to Tokyo,
a Nation's self-appointed, self-annointed antihero.
He claims a forebear battled through the quagmire
                              of The Somme.
Please God the old boy never lived to see his epigon.

Football's a convenience truck for patriotic highs.
Long stay or early exit, he'll drink and smash tavernas dry;
then back to good old Blighty, wife, two kids,
                             a mortgage too,
where terror-stricken neighbours pray
                        for World Cup Timbuktu.

Let the racist be crept up on while sleeping off a blinder.
Let the *surgeon* sever cleanly, leave no root to re-engender.
Let the sod be segregated from his xenophobic balls,
lest he progenate a master race from *tae kwon do*
                        to carpet bowls.

Lunchbreak – Back Garden

It's not pride that sees me stopping here.
Not the Fuchsia that bloomed first time
this year. Not the Virginia Creeper
retrained in November and now in September
a mass of crimson and gold. *Au contraire,*
I'm here for devotions. Twenty minutes
to give thanks for how it sustains me,
tops me up on chlorophyl.

And so much of it a bird-transported,
bird-dropped, wild and wilful,
original thing which takes me away
from an urbane place where I must scheme
to win or lose or hold my own.
But let that be. The birds have come,
flip-flap-fluttering their way
in and out of my communion.

A chaffinch once took bread
from my thumb and forefinger, a trust
between David and a passive Goliath.
I touch butterflies on the Buddleia,
so engrossed are they in their work.
The brush of insects no longer triggers
violence in me (not so indoors).
I can worship here without deference

to any god, acutely aware
that forty feet and two flicks away
SKY news ticks on with religious
injustice, lies and bombs. My ancestors,
too uninformed, too weary, to care,
turned this ground for a living – a passion
my father understood and I ignored.
Am I catching on? Or is it

escapism? That blackbird would say so.
He's stared me down with his gold-rimmed cherry
for fully five minutes and likely more.
OK mate, you win. It's always yours.

A Waste of Space

This man who talks of people skills,
of counselling, of group work,
is out of place with his silver hair

bunched in wisps around his ears,
in his torn jacket and ravished brogues.
An oddity. A waste of space.

Can't do an attachment
to an e-mail. Forgets his password
and other crucial things.

When told he's out of touch,
has the nerve to ask from what.
Bins most of his e-mails, then he

switches his computer off!
Stares too much at his tank
where goldfish circumnavigate

his ignored and scattered paperwork.
What good could possibly come
from all that faraway thinking?

These middle-aged people
who visit with their thanks
for his help in ages past

are such a hindrance.
We do things differently now.
It won't be long. He's due

to go, go tend that garden
he's always digging and where
he writes his crazy poetry.

We'll put a state-of-the-art
communications system
in his untidy old berth.

Of Faith and Truth

Without even thinking to ask me
in whom or what I believe,
the Baptist minister says to me:
The peace of Christ be with you.

When Pizarro handed a bible
to the Incas, it wasn't a gift.
They declined, declaring their creator
was the Sun, for which he killed them.

Posthumously,
they won the support of Galileo
who renounced his unshakeable science
when threatened with holy torture.

Newton and Darwin are in Westminster Abbey,
laid there by a Christian race
for shedding light where darkness
thrived on fear and obedience.

It's been a long hard road. Still is.
For what is the Baptist thinking?
That I'm a devout believer
or a sinner worth redemption?

Just Scotland: for John Bennett

Let me be thankful for how it is,
not subscribe to clubs who mock
the shyness, dourness and understatement
of our race or disown its alter ego
when exploding on the barley.

And save me from aficionados
of Victorian embroidery:
let me saunter through Braemar
not entering a single gift shop,
take an untramped whisky trail

by loomlike agitations
and recitations of running water:
let me chance on a deer off guard,
or a curiosity of newborn lambs,
or a pheasant who's forgotten why she's there:

let me wander the old Capital,
past secretive close and high stepped roof,
straining uphill, resisting downhill,
then cross Princes Street to be steered
by the military squares of Georgiana:

let me stay in a patriotic hotel,
checked in by a Dutch receptionist,
served wine by a Spanish waiter,
and not hear parlance till black
pudding is asked for at breakfast.

Respecting the past but shot of the luggage,
and turning a deaf ear to MSPs
bumping their gums on crazy targets,
let me travel with my own mind
from indifferent moor and rugged upland

to the auto-teller and IT city,
from small cairn to tall monument,
with no pipes and drums in my head,
without piety, privilege or judgement,
in this my country.

A Diplomatic Day

To the sounds of falling water,
a bumble bee and cabbage white,
thirty three and one third years

go flapping, buzzing, babbling by
in the alternating light and shade
of a garden's afternoon:

three decades plus of carousel,
of up n down, of standing still,
of twist and bust and start again,

of plodding horses, creepy crawlies,
ostriches and leaping frogs,
intellects and bureaucrats,

of young cubs, foolish but brave,
bringing light and fire once more
to a dab hand's less dynamic days,

and umpteen thousand punters,
the who and why of it all
(Please God I kept the faith) ,

of schemes fantastic gone agley,
of honest graft and feats unsung,
an oddball stew now boiled down

to the economic word career.
But little will out tonight
in reply to wonderful lies.

Not the first in the seat of honour
to hold his peace and wonder
who it is they're blabbing about.

A day when to be a makar's
no easy warrant. Oh would just once
such licence let damnation loose!

Night Driving

On clear suburban motorways
while the bypassed city snores,
automatic pilot is engaged.
At steady pace, a life reeled back
is read by endless lamplight.

No book however thick could hold
its undisclosed components.
Characters re-appear like old
hitch-hikers from the roadside.
Some good company. Some not.

Two confronting and persistent headlights
return the manual control,
leaving not much recollection
of the last accomplished miles, just those
few established passengers behind.

Poems in Scots

Auld Schuil Tie

Ah hudnae dun ma hamewark,
cuidnae rame ma spellin
neist mornin whun Ah studè up.

She wis a richt crabbit miss,
hurled me roonaboot her
bi the thick end o ma tie.

The knot goat smaaer and smaaer.
Warse, it goat tichter and tichter
Ah thocht Ah wis gonnae choak.

Whun Ah goat hame
ma mither hud tae cut it aff
wi a sherp perr o shears.

Teacher? she gret, *Teacher wis it?*
Dinnae gie me ane o yir lees.
She gied me a slapntheheid,

tellt me, if she tellt me wance
she tellt me a hunner times,
no tae fecht in the playgrun.

And tae think bairns nooadays
cannae spell tae save thirsels
and naebdie gies a damn!

The Other Scottish Game

In a fitba-mental institution
oor heid o classics, no a wan
for playin deid, warked up the gall
ad gloriam familiae
tae introduce the egg-shaped baa.

Eleiven o his *woodenheads*
for wance gained literary cred.
Thir verra manhood bein in peril,
peteetioned thir pretentious maister:
This game is played by poofs and girls.

Syne he took us tae the poshest scuil
and garred us watch dementit bulls
wallowin in muck and rain
then makkin steam, as interlockin
necks wid heave, tak strain.

Wan beast, wha cuidna suffer
wan more slander on his mither,
let fly a blink-and-miss-it punch
wha shifted twa o the offender's teeth
and resurrected lunch.

Nae mair wid thaim as worshipped
the double shuffle, shimmied hip,
silky pass and tap wan-two,
misrepresent the clabbered men
wha shooered doon tae black and blue.

Partners in the Firm

Young John luiked auld. His heid
wis doon it the darg aa day.
Press on! wis aye his bugill caa
whan 'prentices liftit therrs.

Ae mornin, a meenit ahint,
Ah wis stude tae attenshun bi his desk.
He brocht me tae buik and tellt me
tae wark a meenit owre lowsin.

Auld Tam wis unco droll. He jigged
thru the lobby it hauf efter ten,
smirked guid mornin tae ane and aa,
and wap't his bowler (ne'er missed)

on tae the antlert coatiestaun.
Syne he flaucht lik a horn daft bee
for his wee bit comfort plunked awa
whaur naebdie else cuid fund't.

Nane but thaim cuid unnerstaun:
Guid strang wuid, they wir tongue n groove.
Auld Tam pulled the punters.
Young John squerr'd the balance.

Sanctum

Ah tak time in ma back gairden,
the Sin on ma shooders,
oot o the ongoin dingdong,

oniethin tae thole
yon tea-time stooshie efter wark.
It nivir did onie guid.

No sae much a pairt
whaur *Nemo me impune lacessit*
Here naethin fashes me ava –

– gien the skirls o neibours' bairns,
gien *Manic Street Preachers*
oot o an upsterrs windae.

Naethin. Naethin ava.

A blackie coories doon
in the winnlestraes
o a deedback Russian Vine

an, jist lik me,
he gies it laldie
for his ain wee bit scowth.

He 'n Ah are yairds
frae a grand cacophony.
Richt noo it cuid be licht years.

The Blaw

Ther wance wis a boss, a genial man,
wha wis brim fou o vim and gret blawins,
aye said he hud siller for fowk's guidlie plans,
fit in trith nivir wis whaur his mou wis.

Whan it aa cam tae nuthin the clairt
Wis dichtit be a minion he widnae repay.
Gin the top brass wir bayin for bluid,
he'd gie thaim a richt haundy patsy.

Whun the time cam aroond for his push-aff
naebdie wantit tae stage a fareweel.
So he pit oot his ain invitations,
stumped up for a bash it a five star hotel.

He spak for an oor, and then some:
hauf the room wis asleep hauf wey thru.
Whan he feenished, the relief wis sae awesome,
theh jigged the day oot, the nicht too.

Gin ye're in for the long haul career,
beware o fawse promise and blastin.
Tae the gaffer o thrift and leal caundir
ye'll find yirsel pou'd tae in trust.

Moon Pickings, 30th December, 2099

(a play/ poem for two characters)

Hey Wullie, see'z ma lazer scroodrevver.
'Smurder warkin the daurk side pitch

Therr ye go Jim. Nae probs.
Bi the wey, whas hoose is this?

Yon toff – Chairman o *Global Supagrub*
Poozened hauf the Earth's population
in ninety-wan. They stoaped extermination
for that efter The Greens lost pooer.
Bunged him oot here whaur he'd dae
less harm. Dinnae raid the fridge, eh?

Ho ho Jim, you're funny. Bi the wey,
Did the wife cum aff the Christmas Shu'll?

Nae chance. Efter Ah took ma giant leap
for mankind, she split n shacked up
wi an interplanetary estate agent
frae Australia – ye ken, Danunda!
Nae hardship Wull. She hud a face
like a soor ploom wis aye in her mooth.

Ho ho Jim, you're a scream.
My Goad, whit's that? Oh Jesus,
The Space Patrol. We're rumbled!

Ay. But dinnae fash yirsel.
Afore they get roon tae sortin it,
thi'll hae let us oot for aa the
hullabaloo on Hogmanay. Tae get
blootered and bounce aroon Princes Street
– like we dae here, withoot drink.

Ho ho Jim, you're a treat.
Jings, imagine ... A new century.
No the bash it wis last time tho.
Ah remember ma grandfaither tellin me
his faither hud wan o his poems buried
in a capshul. Tae be opened the morra.

Yir great grandfaither a poet? My, Wullie,
zata fact? This must be seen.
Cumoan officer, seez the magnetic hauncuffs
and beam us doon. Sa ferr cop.

Waiting for the World Cup

There was a rain check in debate,
when a tartan-topped, short-skirted barmaid
leaned over for an empty glass:
Dinnae even think aboot it she clarified.

Willie resumed: *Noo Jimmy Johnstone
wis tricky, nae doot, and Bremner wisnae hauf
a terrier, but Jim Baxter, oh man!
Magic. Puir poetry. Ach,* said old Jimmy,
*Youz are no auld enough tae remember
Alan Morton. Ther wis a fitba plerr.*

When time was called, wee Peter straightened,
as best he could on elastic legs,
and puffed out his cheeks: *Yawright auld man?
Ye ready for a wee donner doon the road?
Naw son,* said the sage, *jist caa me a cab.*
Slick as a back-heeled pass, the wee man quipped:

Ah'd rather caa ye Jimmy.

The Portsoy Potter

Doon bi the auld harbour,
roond the back and up the sterrs
frae the gift shop, Ah fund him,
hankled tae the darg, his een

glazed. This man, Ah thocht,
must hae nerves o steel,
rock steddy, nivir a cheep,
and jist twa thumbs movin.

Six and a hauf meenits tae mak
a fruitbowl. *It's guid*
haein a craft Ah said.
He seemed tae like that.

The Richt Respeck

(Langholm Cemetery,
Saturday, 30th September, 2000)

I'll ha'e nae hauf-way hoose, but aye be whaur
Extremes meet - it's the only way I ken
to dodge the curst conceit o' bein' richt
that damns the vast majority o' men.
                                        - Hugh MacDiarmid

It's fower weeks noo sin Ah stude therr.
A poem'll scrieve itsel in its ain
guid time – a rule he'd unnerstaun.

Aside ma faither an auld wumman crawed,
No hauf a character eh? her chowks
ferr lowin wi Border pride.

Ah read frae the lanelie hodden stane
that kythed amang ithers aa makkit o marble,
and smirked whun Ah cam tae *extremes*

The wale o verse did rax ma wits.
But noo Ah see. He didnae hae the braith
tae ring mair cheynges himsel.

Scotland willna flooer lamentin
ower Culloden, nor pauchlin nips
o English gress, nor biggin ither

Holyroods tae pseudo-independence.
Better tae lairn tae be oreeginal
and mak the maist o it.

Sair Teeth

Heid in hauns, a hauf shut knife,
Ah sat i the fit o ma scratcher,
girnin wi girl o the gab.

In the peerin daurk, the nakit trees
wir hingin wi the hauntin lichts
o Leslie Toon ayont, the foremaist

crawlin ower the windae lik a wabster.
thou hell o' a' diseases is a line
frae Burns. Ah ken a new ane:

laist nicht's dirlin twang wis Hell itsel

The Education of Tacker McNab

(Ballade – with chorus for audience)

His ain name wis Colin, a frail kinna lad
and the only assistant thon day tae be had.

Ay we ken, weel we ken,
we ken fine whit ye mean

Guests frae the continent, noo on thir wey,
a flat tae be furnished, a kerpit tae lay:
no lang stertit, ther cam a sherp bleep on the phone
– Ah hud tae shoot aff, leave the laddie alane.

"Noo Colin," Ah said, "here's a new box o tacks.
Jist dab roond the door, ye'll soon get the nack."
Imagine ma shoak cummin back in a flutter
– the hale bluddi kerpit tacked richt tae its centre.

"Ya big dippit scunner, whit a disgrace!"
Rid as a beetroot wis the look on his face.
Ah christened him 'Tacker' – reward for his pains.
And nae mair wis said – so great ma disdain.

Ay we ken, weel we ken,
we ken fine whit ye mean

Noo the tale efter this taks an intrestin twist,
for it seemed noo the laddie cuid scarce ivir miss:
in luv and in life he hud cum tae conclusion
this nickname wis haundy, wi nae limitation.

A lassie, wha luv'd him for the soond o his name,
wis ditched for anithir – he grew fond o thon game.
In the army nae squaddie wid derr tak a stab
o derision it sarjint C Tacker McNab.

Ay we ken, weel we ken,
we ken fine whit ye mean

86

Wis back hame last Tuesday – hudnae seen 'im in years:
"Gonnae be a surjin," – that hud me in tears,
for Ah hope Ah'm nivir his patient in stitches:
likely he'd sew me frae ma chin tae ma britches.

Ay we ken, weel we ken,
we ken fine whit ye mean

Repeat

Guid Scots

Ne'er mind the thrang analysis,
the argie-bargie whit's Scots whit's no,
aa thon lather ower hoo Chris said:

"Dunbar, not Burns!" Ne'er mind
the kilted haggis or the Varsity prof,
hamecomin ex-pats wha bladder on.

Wha kens the hale n stump o it?
Wha's ivir nailed it doon?
Sma tatties aa thon sinderin

in twa. The Plooman and MacDiarmid
wir in thir wey baith richt,
luiked ayont borders tae mankind.

Caitland Isle – Take a Chance

(Australian Shepherd – best in Show, 2006)

Are ye no aa gled
a proper dug wan *Crufts* this year?

Ane wi shanks ye cuid see,
wha cuid rin efter sheep,

wi een leukin intae yir ain
– a coothie, scholarlie chiel,

wi a coatie fine n glentin
and randit like a wattergaw.

No ane o they fru-fru types
wha taks thir gaffer aa day

tae mak up smert, wha reeks
o a winchin laddie's deodorant,

wha taks steps the wey sticks
gaun *mummy daddy* on a drum.

Chance cuid lowp ànd pleh, Ah'll haud.
Guid boy, *Chance*! Braw dug.

Double Standards

Ah sat aside twa cooncillors
at a guid man's fareweel do:
bonnie lassies, service braw,
white table covers and aa.

Dod and Jim, theh yabbered on
abune the ithers heids,
o polis, scabs and pooer cuts,
o picket lines and tories.

Ah cannae staun they graduates,
says Dod wi hertfelt souch.
Nivir bin doon the pit i life,
goat dirt unnerneath thir nails.

Twa oors and mair flaucht by
afore Ah goat an edgeweys:
Ye'll hae tae pardon me. Ah hae
an interview at Cooncil Hoose.

Ach weel, gaes Jim, *ye are weel dressed,*
and ye'll hae dun yir hamewark.
Nae sweat, Ah noddit. *And oniewey*
Ah hae th'important edge:

Ah'm aff tae grab a haunfu o muck,
and push it ahint ma nails!

Wha's Like Us?

Jock Tamson made it tae Holyrood,
loodly sang 'A Man's a Man',
then gied tae genius freedom's haun,
withoot a speir, nae lolly spared.

Scots wham Bruce and Wallace led,
yir girnin's sorely wastit.
Doon in the pit o the Canongate
yir siller cuid be rashly shed.

Scots frae ither nations bred,
yon grand hoose biggit in EH8
wis ower the tap for rinnin late,
and yir cheynge no strang's ye figured.

Scots wham Burns and MacDiarmid lairnt,
gin hypocrisy flooers in Edinburrie,
get intae thon joukerie pawkerie
and scrieve tae yir birse is spent.

Mind tho, wha's like us efter aa?
And dinnae say Jock Tamson's bairns
wid rubbish onie conter opeenions.
It cuid wark oot for best.

Scots bi poet or warrior led,
Scots frae ither nations bred,
welcome tae oor royal abode,
and aa the flummerie!

Oo-be-doo

In the beginnin ther wis her
and ther wis him. She leukit
ower him, and pou'd the nits

oot o his shaggy coat, as perjink
as the day wis lang. And his een
wir stricken wi pleisure.

He leukit ower her, whuther
she wantit it or no, and whun
he wantit his fairins,

weel mebbe, weel mebbe no.
Whiles she'd rin awa, whiles
dunt him wi the branch o a tree.

Nooadays, she straichtens his tie,
dichts the dandruff aff his shooders,
and theh gan oot thegither:

Be caunlelicht and Chianti, he says
aa the richt things, like Romeo
tae Juliet, sclimmin up a vine.

Gin her intimmers are no sae fu,
her heid no sair, he's cantie, for she'll
no rin nor dunt him the nicht.

The evolution o Darwin's darlins
gangs ivir on, but naethin cheynges
atween a wumman and her man.

Vive la Différence

Ten meenits efter last orders,
things wis quate and windin doon.
Or, auld Wullie pipes up:
Ah'm gonnae kill masel.

(A sherp intak o braith aa roond.)
No kiddin he threaps, *Ah'll dae it.*
Whun speired th'obvious, he greets:
Ah've no hud a hard on

for twa year, fower month,
wan week and three nichts.
Tam spat oot a moothfu o beer.
Jimmy fell aff his chair.

Hmm! pits in a heich-heidit dame,
Trust a man to keep a record.
Ahint him the better hauf
hud jist cam in tae drive'm hame:

Ay! And Ah wish he'd 'member
ither days sae weel.

Milestanes

Whun ye wir the cricket o the litter,
ye gowped it me wi goggle een
like Ah wis the eemage o the Lord.

Whun ye turn't tae whit experts caa
an adolescent, ye wir
a prog in ma bahookie,

a soor and thrawn, rauchlin tyke
wi respeck for naebdie, least yirsel.
Ae mornin, we fell oot.

For a whilie yir shaddie
ne'er swippit the doorstane. We didna
hae glent o ane anither.

Syne ye lernt a thing or twa,
and mair besides, oot therr
amang the lions and bears.

And ma newfund scowth, Ah'll tak,
wis snug. Or, whun laneliness
dreeped intae a howe, ma thochts

cheynged. Noo we're speakin (kinda),
speirin it the Warld thegither, ane
auld bletherin skite, ane cannie lad.

Derr We Hope?

(6th September, 2006)

Ah'm no a fitba man these days.
Lang syne Baker and Bryceland
led the line for Saint Mirren.
And lang syne Scotland cuid pleh

wi a cocky snoot – whun Baxter
gied England the rinaroon,
whun the Lawman's heid sclimmed up
tae strike lik a deidlie cobra.

Wednesday lest, tae tak a barley,
Ah saunter't intae an Edinburrie pub.
Ah didnae see the wheen o teles
hingin on aa fower waas, till

twinty vices yowled it me:
"Hey pal, wull ye shift the heid?"
Needin a rinaff afore orderin,
Ah wis hauf wey doon the sterrs

whun Ah goat shot thru wi the blast:
awa frae hame, Scotland hud scored.
And five meenits intae ma diet coke,
theh'd scored again. Ma auld ticker

wis ferr joco. Ah didnae want
tae push aff. But Ah wis meetin
a wumman, ke-en? Oh Scotland,
derr we hope? Derr we?

Demons

Ae drookit morn, twa cats,
black is the ace o spades,
wir sat lik stanes on the gairden waa.

Theh gied me premonitions
sae grusom Ah cuidnae say,
and the twa sphinxes theh wir

ne'er budged nor twitched.
Abune thaim the lift
wis torn intae three bi a fork,

thunder clappit, and Ah saw
a siren in a cutty sark
clingin tae a grey mare's tail.

Ma heid wis spli'in.
Ah wantit tae dee.
And ma wame gaed up n doon

lik an elevator.
Efter twa peels wi watter,
Ah binned the nicht-afore empties,

stuck oot ma tongue
it the gairds o Hell's gate,
and gaed back tae ma scratcher.

Bi the efternin Ah wis better.
Ma pals wir better tae.
The Sin hud cam oot

tae dry and poalish thaim.
Theh leukit guid is new
whun Ah bocht thaim

i' the Gairden Centre.

Targets

They fowk Ah've ayeweys warked for,
wans wi nae job, and young yins
wha kick aroon the streets wi nae
respeck for aubdie nor aathin, are noo

caad *targets* bi the Scottish Exec.
Ah'm tae yaise the loaves and fishes
tae cheynge thaim intae stars and saints
in a twelve month, wid ye credit?

Wan o thaim, jist wan, is makkit
o flesh, bluid, bane and feelin,
thinks his ain wey it his ain raik.
He disnae live in the dreams

o MSPs. Gie's a barley
tae get tae ken the bodie,
and for him, wi aa his luggage,
tae tak the swatch o me.

The Grand Deception

From 1939 to 1945 almost the entire free World was in conflict. As this poem arrives, Iraq has been under occupation by American and British troops for more than half that time

In this warsle o life and daith,
ther's jist no warkin oot
the trith, the hale and nuthin but.

Noo tak this American, wha
wis wance a sojer, sma
and bauchlie, yit cocky wi it,

tae mak up for it, ken,
we've aa met the type.
Goat a thing aboot leftie Islamics,

wants tae punch thir lichts oot,
afore they pit oot hees.
Goat wan fit in Iraq,

jist tae mak shair, tae stoap thaim
pooderin the USA, aince theh fund
the required ammo acoorse.

But heh! Hus embdie clocked
the cost o petrol gaun doon?

Much Cheynged

Fifteen year sin ma dear mither
fell aff this mortal threid, and me
nae mair a Springheeled Jake masel.

The charabang gaed douce, deid slow,
thru aa they fremmit like roads,
and naethin Ah saw Ah kennt.

Mair n wance Ah hud tae stoap.
Expectin nems o pubs, aa Ah goat
wis *Straicht on for fower whirlies,*

*then richt it Tescos and ye canna
miss* Well Ah did, yeah?
Stoaped again tae ask an auld wife:

*Sorry son, Ah've only steyed here
twinty year masel.* Ah wis aa weys
roond the hooses, nae pun inten'it.

Still, whun the Sun cam oot,
the Tail o the Bank dried oot,
and cross the Clyde the hills

wir skinklin wi gold.
Aathin in sicht wis sherp
and the auld BP cam doon.

Ah felt ma feet gan hivvy
and takin root i the tarmac.
So whaur wis the mist frae noo?

New Year's Resolution

It disnae pou ma chain:
twinty-six e-mails ivry mornin
aa cluckin the sem auld sang.

It widnae be sae bad
gin twa or three o thaim
mad a modicum o sense.

Ah'd like tae e-bin the loat.
Aa this bumbazlin PC leid
wull see me tae the funny farm.

You can get it on *fish*
or *one world*, you know?
Just *right click* then *left click*

Ay! Afore Ah dae the hokey-cokey
and turn aroon? Gie's peace.
Then gie me the e-mail hame

o somedie wi the brains
tae ken the difference atween Cyberspeak
and the langwyj o Shakespeare.

If no, the Hell wi it. Ther's jist
five mair months tae go.
Jingle Bells tae yin and aa!

Glossary of Scots

acoorse	*of course*
ae	*one*
ava	*at all*
barley	*moment, break*
bauchlie	*stockily built*
biggin / biggit	*building / built*
birse	*anger and frustration*
bladder	*blether, rant*
bletherin skite	*person talking nonsense*
blootered	*drunk, legless*
bumbazlin	*bamboozling, mystifying*
bunged	*transported, exiled*
cantie	*up for it, hopeful*
chowks	*cheeks*
clabbered	*spattered with mud*
clairt	*mud*
conter	*opposing*
coories doon	*settles down to rest*
coothie	*cute, smart*
crabbit	*ill tempered*
crawed	*boasted*
cricket o the litter	*youngest child in family*
cutty sark	*short smock / undergarment*
darg	*work, toil*
dichts	*wipes, dusts down*
ditched	*jilted, dropped*
dippit	*brainless, stupid*
donner	*stroll, short walk*
douce	*quietly*
drookit	*very wet, drenched*
dunt	*strike, hit*
fairins	*reward, just deserts*
fashes	*troubles, worries*
fecht	*fight*
fit	*which*

flaucht	*flew*
flummerie	*extravagance, excessive show*
fremmit	*unfamiliar, strange*
gaffer	*master or mistress*
gairds	*guardians*
girl o the gab	*toothache*
glent	*sight, glimmer*
glentin	*shiny*
gowped	*stared*
hankled	*harnessed, chained*
hauf way hoose	*compromise, middle ground*
heich-heidit	*snobbish, aspirational*
hodden	*ordinary, plain*
horn daft	*demented, crazy*
howe	*deep hole, depression*
intimmers	*stomach, bowels*
joco	*uplifted, excited*
joukerie pawkerie	*dishonest doings (of money)*
kythed	*stood out*
laldie	*very loudly (of singing)*
lather	*fuss, endless argument*
leal caundir	*plain candour*
leid	*language*
lift	*sky*
lowin	*glowing*
lowsin	*finishing time*
mou	*mouth*
or	*until*
pauchlin	*pinching, stealing*
peerin	*murky, gloomy*
pentit	*painted*
perjink	*painstakingly, fastidious*
pitch	*working patch*
plerr	*player*
plooman	*ploughman (Robert Burns)*
plunked	*stashed*
pooderin	*blowing up, demolishing*

pou'd tae	*drawn*
prog in ma bahookie	*thorn in my backside*
quate	*quiet, subdued*
raik	*pace*
rame	*recite*
randit	*coloured*
rauchlin tyke	*badly behaved person*
rax	*test, exercise*
sclimmed	*climbed*
scowth	*freedom, one's own space*
scrieve	*write*
scuil	*school*
siller	*money*
Sin	*Sun*
sinderin in twa	*splitting hairs*
skinklin	*sparkling*
skirls	*yells, giggles (of children at play)*
souch	*sigh*
speir	*question, confront*
stooshie	*quarrel, argie-bargie*
swippit	*swept, cast itself across*
syne	*soon, so, then*
tak a barley	*take a break*
tak the swatch	*get the measure*
thrang	*controversial, fraught*
thrawn	*bad tempered*
threaps	*moans, complains, goes on*
wabster	*spider*
wale	*choice, selection*
wame	*belly, stomach*
warsle	*struggle*
wheen	*large amount*
whirlies	*roundabouts*
winchin	*courting*
winnlestraes	*withered stalks*
yaised	*used*
yowled	*shouted, bawled*

ISBN 142512929-3